MW00975316

P.L.A.Y.E.R.'S CIRCLE
"REAL MEN ONLY"

Published by The 17th Letter Inc.
Copyright ©2011 by Tiy-E Muhammad

Edited by Jackie Ernst
Book Design by N.C. Bell Design / Nick Bell

For more information:
The 17th Letter Inc.
645 W 9th Street Unit 110-281
Los Angeles, CA 90015

ThePlayersCircle@Gmail.com
www.drtiye.com

ISBN 9780967030708

Printed in the United States of America

10 9 8 7 6 5 4 3 2 1

DEDICATION

This book and my life is dedicated to GOD (The Most High, The Beneficent, The Merciful). Thank you Father for this fifth book. I pray that you continue to use me as a vessel to enlighten the masses. I honor You, I respect You, I fear You, and I give total praise to You. Without You, there would be no me.

～ God is Great

SPONSORS
(Thank you for supporting my vision.)

Platinum level
A. Quran, Aajee', Qayyim
1. Tracey "OCT" Phillips
2. Myron "Magic" Giggua
3. Pamela Kubeczka
4. Carol Blackman
5. Darice Goodwin
6. Ira Watkins
7. Monique A. Wright

Gold level
1. Laverne "Gu-Gu" Gray
2. Annette Dean
3. Casandra Lawrence-Talmadge
4. Joy Johnson

Silver level
1. Ricky Davis
2. Sebastian Wolski
3. Malik Emir-El
4. Shermaxx
5. Cortez Charles
6. Victoria Hubbard
7. Gray/Glaze Family

INDEX

P.L.A.Y.E.R.'S CIRCLE (Vol. 1)

I. PREFACE

Player, a word that is as ambiguous as love, has swept this nation for the past eight decades. His ambiance and savoir-faire persona has intrigued and captivated the desires of every woman who can see him, smell him, and hear him speak.

Yet the word "Player" has never truly been defined. Depending on whom you ask, you'll get a different definition. Some use it as a positive label, while others say it has a negative connotation. Geography also plays a role here. Depending on what neighborhood you were cradled in, the truth behind the word will be interpreted differently. In my neck of the woods (Chicago's Southside), Player was a title every young man strove to embrace. It meant you were the coolest of the cool, the sharpest of the sharp, and you were a monument of self-respect and pride.   Growing up, a Player is what I strove to be.

Being a Player meant you were great at what you did. Be it your business, craft, the way you dressed, the way you treated the ladies, if you were a Player, it simply meant that you did it remarkably well. You were cool, you were accomplished, you were smooth. You were revered by the boys and desired by the ladies. In the neighborhood, it didn't matter what your business was: barber, janitor, gambler, ball player, preacher, schoolteacher, lawyer, mechanic, etc. were all considered Players if they were great at what they did. Player meant you had respect and respect equates to power.

When a man spoke to another man and his first words were, "What's up Player?" it expressed respect and appreciation for the Player and the authenticity of his persona. Women didn't run away from Players; they ran to them.

Today, the concept of the Player has taken a huge turn for the worse. Sometime over the past two decades, men have managed to turn a word of beauty and respect into a word associated with shame and distrust. I am writing this book to redeem this word and to redefine the role of men in the 21st Century relationship. I am writing to set the record straight and to bring my brothers (Black, White, Hispanic, Native American, etc.) back to their rightful place, a place where a man knows his business and knows how to treat a woman, where he is given the space to be great, and he can reclaim his due respect and proper title.

Every woman reading this book, please give it to your significant other and encourage him to read it. If he calls himself a Player, hold him responsible for the content of this book. Because this book was written by a "True Player."

It is with pleasure and integrity that I redefine and place complete ownership on the concept, usage, definition, and knowledge of the word Player in these pages.

Player is not a look, it doesn't have an age requirement, it doesn't have scent, and it can't be bought. Player is simply energy. And just like "sexy," you either have it or you don't.

II. INTRODUCTION

"The game never changes, only the players." False!
I use to think this statement had validity and truth,
but it doesn't. Over the past two decades the game
has changed drastically, and changed for the worse.
Somehow, the True Players of the game forgot to pass
the "How To" book on to the next generation, leaving
most modern day men in limbo, drowning without a
life preserver.

Unfortunately, men are no longer taking pride in being men. There used to be an inherent sense of pride
in the word "man," and the presence of a man com-
manded instant respect. Today's media is doing a good
job of emasculating men (portrayed in pop culture as

soft and docile), and women are having a hard time not only accepting but even recognizing "real men," due to the level of doubt propagated in our mindless mass media. It's time that "real men" learn to "tuck their shirts" (exhibit respect for their inner and outer virility) again. No more "sagging" (failing to show respect for the testosterone that created you). Sagging is for boys.

Men use to take pride in using their mouthpiece to engage women and win them over with wit and charm. Not anymore. Today, men are opening their wallets and allowing material possessions to validate them, instead of their person. Men are doing more "tricking" (using money, deception, and empty promises to attract a woman) than ever before. There should be laws against "tricking" and men (who should know better) should be punished (barred from the Player circle) accordingly.

I'm not blaming men for their lack of skills, because most men in this modern era haven't been taught the difference between "man" and "male," "Player" and "chump." As a man who does know the difference, it's my responsibility to educate our men on the "Player's Game," aka the "Game of Life."

This manual will provide men with a realistic knowledge base that will help them survive in this relationship-driven society. We're not surviving now because we don't know the objective of the game. Its where-withal has been purposely hidden from most of us since the beginning of time. For example, a woman will have you believing you're running the game or being a super Player, while all along she's playing you like a Ferris wheel at a carnival, spinning you in circles. One of the greatest tricks ever played on mankind is the proliferation of the notion that men are smarter than women. Women lead you to believe this idea, when in reality women strategically plan and control your every move.

Millions of women across the world are waking up daily asking, "Why can't my man do right?" The answers are both ambiguous and gravitas in nature, and yet the best known sociological response is, "Men don't know any better." Most men are totally ignorant to the small intricacies necessary to satisfy even the most low-maintenance woman. Men are not born with a relationship-chip planted in their brains. We survive instinctively, like infants, for most of our lives, always looking for a breast to suck on and a TV show that doesn't ask us to think about what's really going on in the world.

In this book, I'm pardoning all males. Most of us were born without adequate male role models to help us explore the many facets of relating to the opposite sex.

Men are raised to honor women for one purpose, and once that purpose has been served, the average male ventures off to the next conquest. We mean well, but our good intentions are not enough. We've survived in ignorance for thousands of years.

Men, this book is written so you can understand what's never been taught to you by your absent Player role models (fathers, uncles, scout leaders, school teachers, church advisors, etc.). Ladies, this book will give you an adequate depiction of a Real Player's psyche. If your man isn't performing or your son doesn't have a male role model, this volume will serve as an instrumental tool of higher learning.

Who am I to write this book? A certified Player, who desires to set the record straight. It's time that males stand proudly again and accept their roles as real men in our society. Notably, I've been blessed with an innate ability to understand the Player's game. I know most women better than they know themselves and I've accepted (not to be confused with understand) the ambiguous plight of the female.

The Player's game is not rocket science, and there's no ten-step program to guide you to it or through it. The game is merely an energy that can be obtained through careful observation of one's self and the woman.

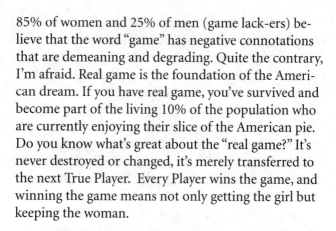

85% of women and 25% of men (game lack-ers) believe that the word "game" has negative connotations that are demeaning and degrading. Quite the contrary, I'm afraid. Real game is the foundation of the American dream. If you have real game, you've survived and become part of the living 10% of the population who are currently enjoying their slice of the American pie. Do you know what's great about the "real game?" It's never destroyed or changed, it's merely transferred to the next True Player. Every Player wins the game, and winning the game means not only getting the girl but keeping the woman.

Since the beginning of time, man has had an innate desire to understand and master his greatest strength and his greatest weakness: the woman. Men have searched through valleys, streams, deserts, high rises, low rises, and the streets of every neighborhood in the world. Yet there has been no discovery of an antidote potent enough to help him master his woman and the pursuit of relationship happiness.

Most prisons are filled with men whose incarceration had something to do with proving their male prowess in front of a woman. When you see a guy fighting in a club, it's not to prove how tough he is for his boys, but how tough he is for the girl. If you'll take notice, most fights between men take place when there are women around. No different than two rams bumping horns to prove who's the brawniest; they do it not for each other but for the lady ram standing near by. And guess who gets the lady ram? The ram left standing, not the sorry excuse for an animal lying wounded on his defeated ass.

When you look at the leaders of our Fortune 500 companies, our NBA All-Stars, the NFL, the MLB, the NHL, our preachers, lawyers, doctors, etc., you can easily see that their ultimate aim is the ultimate trophy: the woman. Most men won't admit this, but everything we do is to impress and sexually conquer the woman. From the time the man steps into his first classroom, he begins his relentless search for recognition from his desired counterpart, the female.

What do you think male competition is all about? It's not to impress his testosterone producing counterparts, but to stand as a king before every woman that he encounters. Most men watch sports not because they are truly fans of the sport, but because they want to emulate the star of that team. There is not one man who didn't want to be Michael Jordan in his prime. Why? Because every woman wanted to have a piece of "Air Jordan." The celebrity represents power and with power, most men know they can have any woman in the world. I said it, "In the world."

If you don't know yourself, you will never qualify to be a Player. Self-knowledge and awareness exude confidence, and confidence is 90% of the game. Confidence is not to be confused with its archenemy, cockiness. If a man is cocky, it's usually a sign that he's lacking true confidence, therefore he uses an outer shell (cockiness or arrogance) to hide his true coward self.

Women often win at the Player's game because they observe men closely, and learn their weaknesses and strengths. A smart woman can plan your rise or demise at any moment she chooses. You, on the other hand, think your dick is the key to the golden gate. Wrong! The key to this whole game is accepting the fact that every "Real Woman" you desire is uniquely defined, and her blueprint is second to none. You can't say you know the Player's game and then treat all women the same way. Women are like snow flakes; they descend from the heavens and no two are alike.

If you the Player develop the patience of a woman, and learn to observe like a woman, you will master this game. Women are like chess players on a mild summer day, while the average man is playing checkers in the winter, excited to make his move because he fears the cold. Every man must know his power-potential. The woman knows and appreciates her powers and she's damn good at using them.

Mental control is the primary objective of the Player's game. Sex is secondary. Any man can get sex, but it takes a Player to possess a woman's mind, sure that the body will follow. Men beware: a woman will give you sex so you think you have control, while all along she's running the program.   See, women know men want sex in the morning, afternoon, and evening. Even if we can't have it, we think about it 90% of the day. Why do you think the term Player exists in the first place? Simple. Every man wants to be recognized as a member of an elite group that can have sex with any woman he desires, at any given time. So he believes.

As any True Player will tell you, if you believe you can truly possess a woman, body and spirit alike, then you've mastered the game. The game boils down quite simply to "The moves that one must make in order to achieve one's objective." In this game, the objective is the woman. It's an unyielding desire that's innate in every heterosexual man. We crave women like bees seek honey. In order to tap into this sweetness, men must follow the rules of the game. If you talk to her, touch her, hold her, kiss her, listen to and adore her, eventually you will possess the woman you most ardently desire.

III. PURPOSE

The goal of this manual is to help men around the world develop better relationships with themselves. Possessing a strong love for the self will grant every man a keener understanding of how to treat his woman. But you have to love yourself first. You can't be a Player if you don't have your shit together.

The ultimate aim of Volume 1 is to encourage Players to become better men, fathers and husbands. Being a Player requires knowing how to treat a woman and maintaining longevity with her. If you're a so-called Player and you've been single and childless all your life, you're the one being played. Marriage is the greatest institution on God's earth, and without your woman by your side, you have not completed your Player-cycle here on earth. When I speak of marriage, I don't mean a formal ceremony before a priest, rabbi or other religious leader, but a spiritual union before God. It's not about the trimmings of a ceremony; it's about two hearts willing to beat as one. If you have a good woman in your life, treat her well and become the ultimate Player, the Player that's married.

In order to best serve you, I have broken this process down into three stages, each with its own unique and enlightening manual.

Volume 1 will explain and give direction on how to become a better and more secure man.

Volume 2 will discuss intimacy and sex.

Volume 3 will discuss marriage and its true purpose.

CHAPTER 1

DEFINITION OF A P.L.A.Y.E.R.
(21st Century)

P. PLEASING
L. LADIES
A. ALL
Y. YEAR
E. EXCELLENCE
R. REQUIRED

A Player is simply a man who recognizes the game of love, sex, and companionship. A Player is NEVER defined by the number of women he can have at one time, but by how he treats the woman he's with at the current moment. You can have several women at once if, and only if, you treat each one like she's number one. And only if you're honest. If you haven't discussed commitment, then there's nothing to discuss.

But if your woman asks you if she's the only one, a Player is always straight. And if she asks you to let her be your only one, then be true to your word or walk away. A Player never misleads a woman. He does not mentally or physically abuse women, either. He's honest with his intentions and responsibly uses his powers to enhance, not hinder.

FYI: There is an enormous difference between being a Player and playing a woman. Playing with a woman's emotions, expressing false intentions, deliberately misleading her affections, misusing her finances, and manipulating the relationship in any way for personal gain, are all examples of playing a woman. It's never good to play with another human being. Playing with a person can lead to death, physical and mental abuse, incarceration, and years of bad karma. As the laws of attraction state, "You will reap what you sow."

Having laid down the basics, let me now explain the six different levels of Player.

Starting at the bottom and working our way up, we'll begin with the "Player Hater."

6. The **"Player Hater,"** aka "coward," is the scum of the Player world. The Player Hater can't be defined as a man, because he's actually a woman trapped in a man's body. This chump is a disgrace to the game and has kept real men from progressing since the beginning of time. Just like the devil hated on Adam, the Pharaoh hated on Moses, Judas hated on Jesus, Jesse Jackson hated on President Obama, and the PGA hated on Black golfers, the coward hates on True Players. You get the point.

Real men don't hate on one another. If you see a man handling his business with a woman, you appreciate it and you keep it moving. More especially, you keep your damn mouth closed. There's nothing worse than a Player hater that goes to a woman and says, "I think you're a good woman and I don't want to see you get hurt. The truth of matter is, your man is cheating on you and you deserve better. If you were my woman, I would never mistreat you that way."

To every man who has displayed this act of Player-treason, you deserve to have your ass whooped. If you've done this in the past, here's your warning: **DON'T DO IT AGAIN.**

A real Player does not have a problem with you stepping to his woman. But real Players do have a problem when you're not doing it on your own merit. Keep the other man's name out of your mouth. If the woman digs you, she'll make the necessary adjustment to be with you.

FYI: Players don't gossip about one another. If you see a stud that's good/great at academics, sports, styling, lady-magnetizing, if he drives a nice car, dances well, sings with his whole soul, don't bad mouth him. Congratulate him and keep it moving. If you have nothing good to say about a Player, it's mandatory that you keep your mouth shut. Never get mad at a Player that your woman chose over you. Your woman made that decision, so step up your game and keep it moving.

5. The **"Stadium Player"** has no idea what's going on around him. He's in the stadium with a box of popcorn and a soda and doesn't have the slightest idea that the woman next to him, who he just met and bought a hot dog and a beer for, is actually giving it to her boyfriend sitting next to her. The Stadium Player is a mental masturbator and social misfit who doesn't possess the courage or the skill set to get in the game. He hides in his virtual world, lurking around social networking sites, and would rather watch porn and play with himself than seek true companionship with a real woman.

4. The **"Bench Player"** is nothing more than a spectator wearing a uniform. He is a member of the team, but no one knows his name or his number. The Bench Player is probably the biggest impersonator known to the Player game. He disguises himself in the uniform of a real man, he talks and walks like a real man, but as his title implies, he never leaves the bench. Maybe last year he was a Stadium Player, and has moved up the Player ladder through careful observation or getting his heart shot to pieces. Maybe he understands the virtue of having a uniform on and going into the game. But the Bench Player still doesn't have the necessary skills to join the game. All he has is his notepad, and he's taking the necessary notes from the bench. Most men with adequate male figures in their lives start out as Bench Players.

3. The **"Recognized Player,"** or the "6th Man," is the Player that has just joined the game. He's not a starter, and by no means an all-star, but he gets respect from the team as a valuable Player nonetheless. Women notice him even when he's not in uniform, and he's developing his "swagger," aka confidence. The Recognized Player comes into the game when the other Players are tired or injured. He does his best, hoping to one day be a starter. He's in a good place because he's finally being recognized, which means he now has potential star power.

2. The **"Signature Player"** is the Player that every man wants to become, but this is also the Player that gives the game a bad name. He's flashy and arrogant. He knows he's the man and strives to nail every woman he can get. Doesn't matter what she looks like, who she is, or how she presents herself. The only requirement for the "Signature Player" is a vagina. The Signature

Player signs autographs and he brags to his boys about his conquests. He brags not to put himself above his peers, but to let the non-alpha males know that their women are never safe around him. And in most cases, the above statement is true. Women are always drawn to the strong and confident man. If she wanted a bitch, she would date a woman. Wherever the Signature Player goes, he takes pride in his ability to get any woman he chooses. His sex game is second to none, and he admires and welcomes the challenge of the most difficult catch of all, the "Super Diva."

1. The **"Royal Player,"** or "True Player," is second to no Player and truly the star Player on the team. We'll compare him the "point guard." In basketball, the key player on the team is always the point guard. Without a skilled and confident point guard, a team never makes it to the championship. Only the Royal Player ever truly wins the game.

The Royal Player has a swagger that ignites a room upon his entrance, but he's neither boastful nor intrusive. He doesn't need to brag. He knows he's a lion and he waits for his woman to select him. In other words, he has a quiet and powerful pride. A real woman will always select a True Player because he's not thirsty, or anxious for attention. He knows a woman can smell a thirsty man from a mile away. He also knows that once he's been selected, he possesses true power, and it's only a matter of time before he has her mind, heart, body, and soul.

There aren't many Royal Players around in the 21st Century, because the game has changed and most men are after the body, not the mind. Too many men think that sex with a woman is the paramount achievement. Women today will tell you that sex doesn't guarantee you're in, but if you captivate her mind, you can call at 3 am and she'll jump to make you a sandwich and a fresh-fruit smoothie. As a True Player, you realize that the body is merely an appetizer, but captivating the mind is unlimited access to the buffet at a five-star, all-you-can-eat restaurant.

Players, don't get upset if you're not at number one status. Especially don't hate on the man next to you with number one status. It requires years of training and commitment to the game to be a True Player.

One of the key components to being a Player is always recognizing your strengths and skills, and not disliking or hating on the man who is more skillful than you. The best thing for you to do if you can recognize that you are not on level one is to step up your game. In order to step up, you must practice and most of all respect the game. Let's take Brett Favre for instance (arguably one of the best QB's of all time). He's most admired for his love and passion for the game of

American football. Other players on the team honor him on the basis of his love for the game and prowess on the field. Apply that same logic when dealing with women. You will never understand a woman (that's not your job), but you will be able to accept her and have her fulfill your every wish if you exude your manhood and play the game the way it's meant to be played. Remember, "A woman submits to her man, who submits to God."

CHAPTER 2

THE PLAYER'S APPROACH
(Catch a Girl, Kiss a Girl)

How to Approach a Woman

Every woman is different, but every woman appreciates a respectful and courteous man. When you approach a woman, always start by greeting her with words of kindness. Give her a compliment and let her know that she's beautiful, sexy, gorgeous, and intelligent. But also make sure every word you use comes from the heart. Women can spot a phony from a mile away, so make sure you're authentic or she'll turn away.

After acknowledging her, ask her if you could have a few moments of her precious time. If she says yes, began to engage her with simple words and keep it short. If you're truly interested and she's in your lane, ask her for her number. As a rule, never engage a woman for the first time for more than five minutes. Always respect that she has other things to do and it's best that this conversation continues on the phone, or on your first date. Players don't hem women in at the corner of the club for an hour. This is a bad move and it's usually too much too soon. Get the number and get to stepping.

Let's look at an example.
You're walking and you see a woman that you find attractive. She's walking toward you. Your first step is to speak to her, and ask her how she's doing. If she responds, "I'm fine" and keeps walking, that means she's not interested. For you, this means turn the other way and walk away. You can't have every woman you see, so there's no need to waste time chasing what you know you'll never catch. Don't let your ego get in the way; you'll only be disappointed. Just go after the next woman that fits in your lane.

On the other hand, if she responds, "I'm fine thank you, and how are you?" this is usually an indication that she would like to continue the conversation. This is called the "interview stage." If she likes you during the interview stage, you'll be rewarded with her phone number. If she doesn't like you, you'll probably get her email, Facebook info, or the number one not inter-ested response, "I already have a man."

-Meaningful Dialogue (How to maintain her interest)

Most men have a very limited arsenal of things to talk about when engaging a woman. We get lost after the introduction and can't/don't know how to carry on a meaningful conversation. We make talking to a woman a lot more difficult than it has to be. Believe it or not, she's as nervous as you are. No one like starting over, and men and women alike are a bit word shy during the initial stage.

So Players, listen up. When talking to a woman, the first thing to remember is make eye contact, and then remember to keep at least two to three feet of space between the two of you. You don't want the woman to feel in any way violated or threatened by your presence. If she's comfortable, she'll make sure you're comfortable. Once you've gotten past the name and location segment of small talk, it's time for the meat of the conversation. Conversation pointers:

1. *Compliment her on something she's wearing (not her body).*
2. *Compliment her fragrance. She smells good with the express purpose of attracting you.*
3. *Tell her she has a beautiful smile, hair, teeth, etc. Only give sincere compliments; don't lie.*
4. *If you're in a public place, ask her if she visits often.*
5. *Ask if she's originally from the city the two of you currently live in.*

6. *Talk about places she loves most in the city.*
7. *Ask her what about the last movie she watched.*
8. *Ask her about her favorite foods and drinks.*

The above questions are what I call "lead to" questions. One of the questions is bound to lead to a discussion about other things. If you ask her about the last movie she watched and it was a romantic movie, you then ask her if she likes romantic movies. If she answers yes, you can respond by saying, "I'm going to the movies this weekend to see the greatest romantic movie ever. Are you available to join me?" She'll laugh and ask, "What movie is that?" Your response is, "The one starring you and me."

It's corny, but it will put a smile on her face.

Remember: always allow the woman to dictate the direction of the conversation. Don't get caught up in yourself and your personal accolades. Who cares? Make the conversation 80% about her and 20% about you.

CHAPTER 3

SEX VS. ROMANCE

Sex is one of the major points of this book, and I would be lying to you if I said otherwise. Everyman wants sex. Every man reading this book is hoping to come away from it with a keener insight on how to obtain better sex, more frequent sex, or a greater variety of sexual partners. The sex game is very simple, and if you apply what I'm teaching you correctly, you can have any woman you want, anytime you want her.

First rule of thumb: recognize and accept that you don't control the sexual energy, women do. You control the romance that leads to sex. You are the key and the woman is the ignition. The key (romance) has to fit the right car in order for it to turn. Every woman desires a romantic man, but most men would argue that they don't know how to be romantic. Men, you're digging yourself into a hole with that argument. Each and every one of you has the ability to create romance. To be romantic simply means to tune into and appeal to your loving, caring, and passionate psyche. You must realize that this part of the Player's game helps you to win her heart, and once you've got her heart, her body is yours for life.

It's always the little things that count, the subtleties, much more than the "big" things. It's not about how much money you spend on your woman but the amount of quality time you spend with her. Yes, you can spend money all day long and she'll more than likely give you sex, but as a real Player, you need a woman who submits to your mouthpiece (your ability to say what's needed when it's needed). You need to charm your woman with real romance.

If you don't know how to be romantic, I'm listing a few easy ways to get started. Remember, every woman is different, and has her own ideas regarding what she finds romantic. Woman #1 might love flowers and candy, while woman #2 may hate flowers and candy but love going to the park, holding hands and talking. One thing is certain - every woman loves a genuine man. So even if she doesn't like your particular strain of romance, she'll typically still give you love because you put forth the effort. And as you move forward, she'll let you know exactly what she needs.

10 ways to express your romantic self:

1. *Mail her a card that says, I'm thinking about you, I miss you, I love you, etc.*
2. *Take her to a museum, art exhibit, or jazz club.*
3. *Prepare a meal for her.*
4. *Massage her feet with oils that she likes.*
5. *Buy a camera and take pictures of her. This lets her know you appreciate her beauty.*
6. *Make a CD of her favorite songs and the two of you dance the night away.*
7. *Run her a bath with candles lit and soft music.*
8. *Go to the gym together.*
9. *Go to Barnes and Noble together and have tea while reading.*
10. *Always open her car door (both when she's getting in and when she's getting out of the car). Chivalry is the biggest turn-on for a woman.*

FYI: Women give sex to receive affection, and men give affection to receive sex.

CHAPTER 4

The Female Player
(Prolific Player)

It's only befitting that I grace this book by paying homage to the most prolific Player of all time, the woman. How ridiculous it is for a man to think he has control over something that the woman has mastered from her conception? I don't feel the need to address Eve and Adam, you know the story. But I will help you to understand that everything you think you know, a woman has already thought it. For every dollar you've made in your life, she's made two. For every orgasm you've had, she's already had five. She is without a doubt the Player we all aspire to be.

How could this be, the Player-in-training may ask? The woman is a thinker and a processor by nature. She plans things years ahead of time. She strategizes and plots far beyond the capacities of the male psyche. She can say yes when she really means no, she can say no when she really means yes, and you'll never know the difference. She can smile when she's really crying on the inside and she can cry when she's grinning and glowing inside. In case you didn't know, Player, most women fake orgasm at least 50% of the time. This is not because she doesn't enjoy you, but because she wants you to believe she's enjoying you a lot more than she is in actuality. This minor fraud is enacted to please your ego and she can do it on cue, just like the actress she is.

Every thing that comes out of a woman's mouth has already been processed ten times over before she releases it. She chooses you; you don't choose her. She plans your rise or demise minutes, days, and sometimes even months before you've even noticed she's in the room. She's clever and witty, and wears the most deceptive disguise ever to surface on our earth - a disguise we call "ignorance." Yes indeed, the woman plays the ignorant game like no other. You may think she doesn't know who's in your bedroom when she's not there, or you may think she doesn't know that you gambled your money away and that's the real reason you can't take her on that illustrious vacation you promised, but she knows.

It's all about timing with this witty creature. Like a brilliant public defender, she waits until she has built her case against you, then strikes when you're at your most vulnerable. You're left paralyzed as she begins to unravel the months of investigative work she's compiled. The craftiest part is, she does it with a smile on her face, as if to say, "You fool. You really thought you were smarter than me?"

Player, let me be the first to tell you, you're never smarter than the woman. She chooses to accept your bullshit when she wants you. When she's fed up, she simply leaves without notice.

Let's compare this battle to the game of baseball. The batter (man) comes up to bat anticipating the pitcher (woman) has several pitches she can throw at you (usually three to four different styles). You may think she hasn't faced the caliber of batter you are, but she has. Some have been very successful against her, and others have faltered. Generally, she comes right at you with her best stuff, without attempting to disguise her pitches. In her mind, she has you figured out, and most of time she's correct. She can strike you out if she chooses to throw pitches she knows you can't hit. But instead, she throws your favorite pitch, on purpose, hoping that you'll hit it out of the park. When you hit the homerun, you get the prize. You think you earned it, but in reality, she let you have it.

If you don't hit it, she shrugs her shoulders and thinks, "It's obvious he's not ready for me." Most women will give the common laymen a chance to hit her best pitch, and this is why you'll occasionally see ordinary guys with a gorgeous woman. She threw him her best pitch, probably anticipating he wouldn't come close to hitting it, and when he did, she had no choice but to surrender and open her gates.

What is her pitch? It could be several things. It could be a question she asks, an attitude she strikes, it could be the way she smiles at you, the way she walks past you. And what, you may ask next, inspires this pitch? It could be your swagger, the number of women you approach in the club, it could be your VIP club pass, the car you drive, your intelligent conversation, your ability to make her laugh. There is no standard pitch; the pitch depends on the pitcher, and every pitcher is different. I repeat, every pitcher is different. A Player never approaches different pitchers the same way, and a True Player knows he must change his approach to suit the pitcher. If she wants you, she'll give you the right pitch to hit.

Important to note is that the mother of the average woman educates her on the rules of the game at a very early age. Especially if the mother has some game, and most of them do. If you really want to know your woman, pay careful attention to her mother; she'll give you all the missing pieces to the puzzle, and that's a guarantee. If the woman you're pursuing is a club girl, sorority girl, has an abundance of female friends, watches a lot reality TV, frequents strip-clubs, drinks or smokes a lot, is a business owner, has older brothers/sisters or immediate male influences, or if she's a part of the TV, radio, or movie industry, please believe she has game, she knows the game, and she plays the game.

The "Prolific Player" (woman) is so skillful she will purposely instigate a fight with you to provoke your emotions on one end and to dismiss herself from you on the other. That's right, your woman will come to you and pick a fight about the smallest issue simply so she can build up the courage to walk away from you. When a woman knows she's in a bad situation, she won't walk away drama free. She has to create a situation that makes her feel emotionally empowered first, and only then is she able to walk away. Everything a woman does is perfectly planned and executed. I tip my hat to all women. Play on, Players!

Women have girls' nights out, tea parties, get-togethers, sleep overs, spa days, book clubs, vacations, etc. for a reason: to build their strategies and take notes from veteran Players in the game. Even if the woman doesn't know the other woman, she respects her experience and knowledge. Women, unlike men, listen to each other, and most of their plans work, because they possess the "It" factor that most men lack (intuitive knowledge of how the power dynamic in a relationship works).. Which makes us simple, gullible, and dumb as rocks.

If you don't believe the above paragraph, I want you to think about the last time you heard a woman disagree with another woman to her face; you haven't. Women have an unwritten code that it's them against every man. While men attempt to receive brownie points for disagreeing with and even humiliating a fellow Player in front of a group of women, this tactic merely empowers the women and emasculates the Players. On the contrary, women will go to great lengths to show love to one another, even when they feel another woman is wrong. They're smart Players, a lot smarter than they initially may seem.

Players, never dishonor the male code in front of women. If a fellow Player says something you disagree with, you wait until the two of you are alone and then you set the record straight.

The next scenario will give you examples of how cunning, persuasive, and opportunistic most women can be. In other words, women are the greatest liars on the face of the earth. If they want it, they will get it, and they'll use whatever tactics necessary to obtain and secure the desires of their hearts. If you don't believe me, go ask your father or any male figure close to you how he ended up married. I'm certain the story will end with, "She calls all the shots and I just do what I do to keep the fuss down."

And if you think that motherhood tames a woman, think again. Becoming a mama only helps a woman climb to the next rung on the ladder of Player-dom. Want proof? Just consider the following real-life scenario.

Victoria is a beautiful dancer who pokes holes in the condoms she uses with her richest, sexiest clients. Platinum-selling rapper Malik is no exception. Victoria lures him to her bed and this time, her plan works, and she finds herself carrying the child of her dreams, the child who will guarantee her a VIP pass to the realm of super-stardom and funding for the next eighteen years. But nine months later, Malik refuses to recognize his son, despite the outcome of paternity tests and long court battles. Before you say "Poor Victoria," take a moment to meet Maurice.

Maurice is a Stadium Player. He's been waiting his whole life to meet a knockout like Victoria, and when he finally does, he doesn't have a clue about the rules of the game. Victoria can smell a sucker from a mile away. Over the course of three years, she gives Maurice sex a whopping total of two times, and in return she gets her bills paid, her pockets filled, her son taken care

of while she dances for other men, and more dia-
monds than she ever wanted in the first place. Best of
all, Victoria retains total freedom, so she can window
shop for Mr. Right while Maurice holds down the
financial fort. In other words, because Victoria knows
the rules of the game and Maurice doesn't, Victoria
graduates to Royal Player status while Maurice can
only pant with joy to be her royal bitch.

CHAPTER 5

PLAYERS' LANE
(Stay in Yours)

There are many rules to the Player's game, but there is only one essential rule that applies without compromise. That rule is "Stay in your lane." All True Players understand and abide by this essential rule until death.

You may be wondering what I mean when I use the word "lane." Well, take a look at your social-economic status, religious affiliation, political beliefs, personal style, sexual preference, social hangouts, friends, education, personality, car, living quarters, etc. These are the factors that define the "lane" you are driving in. Now apply that to relationships. You should not only be aware of your own status, but should judiciously select a woman that is compatible with and realistically obtainable by someone of your status.

Staying in your lane is very simple: Approach women who are in your line of attraction and who will find you attractive in return. Don't try to score chicks who you know are out of your league; it's a waste of your precious time and energy. You can compare staying in your lane, with trying on a pair of sneakers. You know what size you wear, but you may choose to go a size larger and compensate by wearing two pairs of socks. Not good. True Players will only wear shoes that fit, and if a store does not have his size the Player will go elsewhere. The same rule applies to the woman you're sizing up. If she has the potential to join your team (the right height, weight, hair style, complexion, degree of sex appeal, etc.), recruit her and enjoy the ride. But if she's not what you're looking for, don't waste her time or your time. A True Player allows the Player that's a better fit for the female to have the female.

The Player recognizes the type of women he's attracted to, the type of women he attracts, and what environments are conducive for his selection process. There's nothing more irritating to a woman than when a man who is not on her level (and knows it) pursues her as if they are riding in the same lane. Am I saying you can't have any woman you desire? I am not. I'm saying that every person on this earth has a dating pattern, or lane, that they should be aware of and stick to under all circumstances. There is no reason to deviate from this pattern, as there is plenty of female traffic in your lane, waiting to be hailed down by a Player like you. Stay in your lane and you'll have great success in the dating realm.

When you're successful in your realm, every so often you'll receive a gift. A gift is a woman whom you never expected to attract and who is suddenly in your lane, driving right beside you. Most of the time you'll find out that she was in your lane from the beginning, you just failed to see her. In laymen terms, if a Player considers himself to be B-status, then that Player's game can only captivate B-status women or less (less doesn't mean she's not the quintessential woman; it just means she's not in your lane, so she may not be quintessential for you). Why waste your time going after the unattainable, or the less-than-perfect, when all that your heart desires is already waiting in the lane you inhabit?

Example 1 (What not to do)

Hello, my name is Anthony, and I'm the coolest self-proclaimed Player around. I can have any woman I want, whenever I want her. I have the courage of a lion. I am 5' 11", in fairly good shape, and I have a job working for the city of Chicago. I approach at least two to three women a day, and if I'm turned down 75% of the time, I'm still happy with the 25% I was able to captivate.

I recently met an extremely beautiful woman named Octavia, a former cheerleader for an NBA basketball team. Now it was obvious that Octavia was out of my league, but as long as I kept buying her drinks, I kept her interest. By the end of the night, I even got her math (telephone number). I took her out to dinner and spent more in a few hours than I made in a week, all for a peck on the cheek.

At Octavia's request, our second date was court-side seats at a Chicago Bulls' game that put me out $1000 dollars I didn't even have, and now owe my best friend. When Octavia bailed on me after the game was over, claiming a stomach ache, I was disappointed. When I found out her ailment was a ruse, and that she ended up on the arm of an NBA all-star at a raging after-party, well, that stung. But give up? Never. I know that Octavia will come crawling into my arms once her superstar jock gets bored and moves on to the next set of legs in a short skirt. All it takes is patience, and a C-status Player like me can bring home an A-status female. Patience and a little bit of cash.

Example 2 (What to do)

My name is Alex, and I'm an authentic ladies man. You'll never hear me bragging about my title, but you'll surely see me living it. I live in Los Angeles and I'm a mid-level movie producer. I live moderately and spend a lot of time and energy on my favorite hobby: women. They either love me or hate me. I admit I can be an egotistical, narcissistic, vainglorious jerk, but what you see is what you get.

I recently found myself perusing the goods on display at the Beverly Center Mall, and came across a woman with the face of an angel working at the Foot Locker. Her nametag read Darice, and when I spoke her name and asked if she had plans on Friday, her breathy, "I'm available" assured me this woman was mine.

We ate dinner in West Hollywood, and then we grabbed a few drinks at a local bar that Darice, my angel, recommended. Coincidentally, it was around the corner from her apartment, and it wasn't long before Darice was drunk and inviting me back to her place.

It didn't take her thirty minutes before she was tearing off her clothes, and I have to say, I was into it. But once my pants came off, Darice wasn't feeling it. Her head was spinning and she needed to breathe. Then she needed to talk. Darice told me she was an aspiring actress, and really needed help getting her foot into Hollywood's door. If that wasn't enough, she started crying and going on about how she couldn't pay her bills and was $1500 short of meeting rent for the month. It was truly one of the best performances I've ever seen.

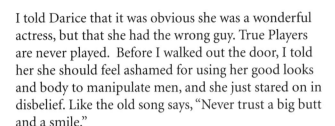

I told Darice that it was obvious she was a wonderful actress, but that she had the wrong guy. True Players are never played. Before I walked out the door, I told her she should feel ashamed for using her good looks and body to manipulate men, and she just stared on in disbelief. Like the old song says, "Never trust a big butt and a smile."

Now that you've read the two above examples, let's take a minute to analyze and discuss. Anthony is very excited by the idea of sex with a beautiful lady, but his expectations are unrealistic. He doesn't respect his lane, and he doesn't mind getting mistreated and abused by women, as long as he gets laid in the end. Anthony is the horrid Bench Player who never sees his true potential and thus will never be a True Player. Unfortunately, Anthony will probably have sons who will follow in his footsteps and spend their virile years sitting out on the bench.

In Anthony's example, there are a few things a Player of any level should never do. Never spend money you don't have to impress a woman. Never borrow money from anyone to take a woman out on a date; if you're too broke to date you shouldn't be dating. Thirdly, don't move faster than your legs will take you. Anthony is trying too hard to be someone that he's not, hence, he's not "staying in his lane." Lastly, never spend money on a woman expecting to get sex in return, unless she's a prostitute. Spending money on prostitutes is prohibited and frowned upon by all True Players.

In my second example, Alex uses his intuition and his knowledge of women to bypass the superficiality of looks and therefore he sees Darice for exactly who she is. Alex recognizes that Darice has used her beauty, body, and charm to lure men into her space and misuse them. Darice isn't what we would call a bad girl, but she's a true game stopper, and game stoppers are truly bad for the game. Women like Darice stop potential True Players from advancing to their full potential. Once a Player has been mistreated by a woman like Darice, the Player is in danger of beginning to resent women in general, and that's when the harsh treatment of women begins.

As a Player, you must be able to recognize women like Darice from a mile away. It's not something that I can teach you by way of rules and formulas; it's something you must learn to feel. True Players use instinct to determine what woman is right for them. Instinct is the most powerful tool a Player can use in the Player's game. Always look beyond what a woman is saying and look into her eyes to discover her true self. But in order for you to discover her true self, you must know your true self.

CHAPTER 6

KNOW THYSELF

Mental, physical, and spiritual health are essential if a Player wants to win the game. To be a True Player, you must have a true connection with yourself. You have to be a professional athlete, minister, and genius all balled up in one. You'll need to know the extent of your physical and mental capabilities. This game of love is tough and only the strong survive. So if you don't know yourself, it's easy for a woman to walk all over you, or choose the man standing next to you without thinking twice.

Let's break down the three pillars of Player health. Are you mentally stimulated and engaged on a daily basis? Do you read? How do you prepare for your day-to-day? It doesn't matter what you read, as long as you consume words and information on a regular basis. You have to be knowledgeable about yourself and you have to know what is happening in the world around you. You have to formulate opinions, you have to think. The lion gets respect in the jungle because he knows his terrain. He knows where he can and cannot travel; he's as mentally tough as he is physically intimidating. I'm not saying you need a PhD; education alone is not the name of the game. But intelligence is the masterpiece that all Players must possess. Education is important in that it prepares you to succeed in society, but intelligence is what keeps you alive in the world. Most women are equipped with an enormous amount of intelligence. Women listen and observe, while like the cowardly hyena, men travel about looking and hoping for scraps.

Spend time getting to know yourself. Allow yourself ample hours every day to focus on your goals and aspirations. Women admire men who have a plan of action. It doesn't matter what the plan is, just spend time building toward your future. Being a Player encompasses more than tallying up the number of women you've sexed. A Player's number one asset is his mind, and if you're not mentally strong enough for the game, don't waste time trying to play it. This game is serious and it's left many unprepared men confused, depressed, incarcerated, homeless, bankrupt, suicidal, and dead. The mental power of the Player is not to be dealt with lightly. In the end, it's what will build you up or tear you down and destroy you.

Now let's get physical. Tell me Player, are you in shape? Probably not! What type of shape are you in, if you're calling yourself a Player? Can you run a block without passing out? Do you ever go to the gym or exercise in the park? Can you pick your woman up and take her to the bedroom without passing out? Can you fit into your vehicle comfortably? Can you get out of the bed without scooting to the edge because you're too fat to get up on your own? If you've answered "No" to any of these questions, you are not physically prepared to be a Player.

A Player's most prominent lure is his presentation, his physical attributes. A woman won't give you the time of day to get to know your mind if the physical package is out of whack. The woman has to like what she sees in order to entertain the thought of talking to you.

What are you doing to attract women? Are you attracting women on your own merit, or are you flashing your money to get women? Unfortunately, a lot of men turn to illegal activities to keep up a certain lifestyle to impress the woman. If you have to break the law in order to bring home the woman who has caught your eye, that's a good indication that the game has gone horribly awry. If you're using anything other than your natural assets to attract females, then you're not a Player, you're a sucker. You're making the game bad for True Players. Show off your health, not your wealth, chump.

That said, a Player has to look fine. You don't need an extensive, expensive wardrobe to get a woman, but you do need to look presentable and tasteful when approaching a woman. Wearing an ill-fitting pair of jeans and a distended white t-shirt is not acceptable. You have so-called Players walking around dressing like inmates in a foreign prison. Pull your damn pants up and tuck your shirt. True Players dress with dignity and pride, not like slobs. If you have to hold your pants up with your hand while you walk, that means you're uncomfortable. If I can see your underwear while you're walking, that means I'm uncomfortable. No one wants to see the crack of your ass in the streets. It's important to remember, you are your "walking resume."

A True Player spends time taking care of himself. He wants to look nice in his clothes, and he doesn't have a problem going shopping to buy a few nice pieces to look good for the ladies. It doesn't require a lot of money to look good, but most men don't know what they should and shouldn't be wearing. There are clothes designed for your body type. There are colors that enhance your image. When you walk into a clothing establishment, don't be afraid to ask a female worker what looks good on you and what doesn't. Remember, you're dressing well both to feel good about yourself and to look good for the ladies.

Classy clothes and shoes equate to confidence, and confidence is the secret to getting any woman you choose (in your lane, of course). If you don't have confidence in your physical appearance, your game is over before it starts.

Never shop for the approval of your male friends; they don't matter. If you're looking good to impress men, you should be dating men. Another man's opinion means nothing when it comes to your dress code. Find a woman you respect and who respects the game and ask her what she thinks about your physical appearance. She'll be honest with you. Find at least three women that you respect and appreciate and use their opinions to improve your style and become more physically fit.

If you take care of your body and your mind, and if you respect yourself and the females that you desire, then your spiritual health will follow. These are not exclusive concepts, but are closely interrelated. If you neglect one part of yourself, you are neglecting your whole self.

There are a number things that I can discuss to further solidify my point, but my objective here is to encourage, not discourage. Knowing thyself starts from the time you reach puberty. By that time, you should have a firm grasp on your body parts and their functions.

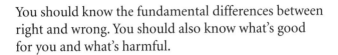

You should know the fundamental differences between right and wrong. You should also know what's good for you and what's harmful.

As a man (Player), you must first know that you're a lion and the world is your kingdom. You were not brought here to be of servitude to any man or woman; you were put here because you're a leader and a great one. You have to appreciate everything about the lion in you in order to maintain the confidence of a lion. A lion never succumbs to weakness, and certainly never behaves like a lioness. A lion knows his role, and he fulfills it flawlessly. A Player can learn a lot from the lion.

I'll close this discussion with some words of advice for you True Players out there. Always be responsible and disciplined. Honor your word to yourself, your family and your community. Be accountable for what goes on around you and the people you love. If you say you're going to do something, stop at nothing to get it done. And always remember who you truly are.

CHAPTER 7

HYGIENE
(Wash Your Ass)

The third biggest complaint (second to cheating and finances) women have about men is hygiene, or lack of it. Men are not washing their asses, and this is a travesty. God (Allah, Buddha, Jesus, etc.) has given you arms and hands for one single purpose: to wash your ass and keep yourself clean.

Players, I'm not trying to insult you, but as men we don't take hygiene as seriously as we should. As they say, "Cleanliness is right next Godliness." You can't right-fully call yourself a Man (Player) if you don't smell the part. Take pride in keeping your body clean and women will appreciate and respect you more than words can express.

I do understand that mothers don't spend a lot of time teaching their young male children how to properly clean themselves, and fathers don't discuss hygiene because most of them have hygiene issues to begin with. Below is a list of the basic essentials to maintaining a clean look. Remember: your body should always be cleaner than your car.

1. Bathe

Depending on your body type (know thyself), you may require two baths a day. One in the morning before you start your day, and one at night before you go to sleep. If you're a constant sweater or your body excretes an odor more offensive and noticeable than most, you need to take two showers a day, minimum. Don't be afraid of water, or of its closest friend, soap. They're both there to make you a better person.

Your natural body scent is an indication of your diet and exercise. A good diet usually rewards you with a fresh scent. On the other hand, if you eat trashy, your body will smell trashy. So what you need to do is to find a soap that works for your body. Depending on your skin type, you may not require a deodorant soap; it could do more harm than good. Don't go to the store and buy the cheapest soap you can find, either. Soap is to a body like wax is to a car; if it's cheap, you'll have buildup or residue. If it's good, you walk away shining. And don't depend solely on showers; baths are essential at least once or twice a week. Get in the tub and soak for15 to 20 minutes, which will allow your pores to open up and rid your body of toxins. By placing a few teaspoons of baking soda and a full cup of peroxide into steamy hot water, you're on your way to a bath designed to relax and detoxify.

2. Deodorant

Buy it, apply it, and don't leave home without it. Deodorant is an essential applicator you must use after having a bath. Don't put deodorant on to mask your funk. Take a bath and afterwards apply a good deodorant designed for your body type (once again, know thyself). You may need to try different brands before you find the one that's suitable for you. Deodorant is inexpensive and it lasts if it's used properly. Don't buy the cheap brand that leaves a chalky buildup under your arms; this is not attractive to women. It's downright disgusting, especially if you're the type that loves to wear sleeveless shirts, and are constantly putting your arms up for the world to see your chalky buildup.

3. Body Oils or Cologne

There's nothing more alluring to a woman than a man who smells delectable. Good smells are an aphrodisiac to women. Players, there is no excuse for you not to smell good. Oils and colognes are the same price as a happy meal, but last much longer. Go to the neighborhood department store and purchase a bottle of cologne that fits your body type. Not every scent was made for you, so what may work for another Player may not work for you. Body oils are the best, because they're more natural and don't contain alcohol, so they last longer on the skin. The average body oil costs $5-10 and is very effective.

When applying oils, just put a dab or two in the palm of your hand and rub it around your hands, neck, and hair. The best thing about oils is that they are compact; you can keep them in your pocket and use them whenever you need to. But be aware of how much scent you're slathering on your skin. Overuse can be just as offensive as none at all.

4. Grooming

When you're born, the first thing that comes into the world is your head, which is usually covered with hair. Your hair is a powerful tool that's used to attract women. Women love a well-groomed man, and well-tended hair complements who you are as a person. It doesn't matter if you have braids, loks, army cut, afro, or a bald head. As long as you keep it neat and tapered, you're bound to attract women. A Player's hair is his crown, and if your crown isn't right, you're not right. Take the time to go to the barbershop and get your hair cut. If you sport a beard or goatee, make sure it's trim and presentable at all times.

If you can't afford to go to the barber, invest in a set of hair clippers and learn how to cut your own hair. There is always something good to say about a Player who is properly groomed. But grooming doesn't only consist of the hair on your head. You have to keep your private areas groomed as well.

A. Underarms

Keep your underarm hair under control. This is not an area intended for a wild bush to sprout. If you close your armpits and there's hair protruding on all ends, your underarm hair is too damn long. Cut it, but don't cut it bald; you need some hair to protect you from different bacteria that can enter the body. Just trim it so it looks presentable. If you don't understand what's presentable, ask your girl; she'll tell you.

B. Chest Hair

I know some women (not many) find chest hair sexy, so if maintaining a tuft suits your style, use it to your advantage, but don't overdo it. Make sure it's tasteful. If your shirt is unbuttoned and your chest hair is getting more attention than your chest, there's something wrong, and you need to make some adjustments. Once again, don't shave it bald, but do make sure it's presentable to the masses, especially if you're motivated to show it off.

C. Pubic Hair

If you unzip your pants and there's a foul odor there, first and foremost, you need to take a bath. Secondly, look at the condition of the area surrounding your man-piece. If it's undesirable to you, guess what? It's twice as undesirable to your lady. Just like you keep the top head groomed, you have to keep the bottom head groomed. Cut the hair around your penis to make it attractive. You know how good it looks when a woman pulls down her underwear and it's nicely groomed? Give her the same satisfaction; it's only fair. Do not, I repeat do not, cut this area bald. Simply trim it and tame it so it looks present-able. Women who love fellatio will stop at nothing to give you pleasure when your area is well-groomed and smells good. Invest in a pair of hair clippers with guards, immediately.

5. Fresh Breath

Players, the key to attracting any woman, regardless of your social status or lane, is your mouthpiece. Keep your mouth clean and fresh at all times. If she can smell it (bad breath), she can't hear it, and if she can't hear you, you're wasting your time.

There's nothing more offensive to a woman than having a man in her face when his breath is ridiculously stank. Brush your teeth, floss, and use mouthwash before you leave the house. Make sure you have gum in your pocket or a packet of mints, in case you encounter dessert (a beautiful woman); she'll really appreciate you for having fresh breath and a clean mouth. Note to self, you're not keeping your breath clean solely for the woman; this is a mandate for yourself. Cleanliness (fresh breath) is Godliness.

6. Feet and Hands (Manicure/Pedicure)

Many men may find going to a spa less than manly. Wrong! Women love a man who takes care of his feet and hands. Just because you're a man with a construction job doesn't mean you should be around your woman with your feet as crusty as the construction site you work on. The average cost for such services is around $50 for both. It's a wise investment and as a Player, every part of your body must be up to par at all times. Keep your feet looking good and your hands silky smooth, but know where to draw the line. Polish on either is unacceptable. Ask the nail technician to buff your nails and you'll have the desired look that your woman appreciates.

Even more basic is learning how to keep your hands clean. A manicure doesn't help a Player when his hands are caked in grime all the time. The consequences of dirty hands can be far-reaching. For instance, consider a typical man out playing basketball with his boys. He's played for over an hour, slapped countless high fives, caught and passed the ball too many times to count, and has even fallen to the ground. One can assume that his hands are filled with germs and bacteria. During a break in the action, he goes to the restroom and doesn't stop to wash his hands before using the urinal, and he touches his penis with these germy hands for about 15 seconds. Only then does he go to the sink and wash his hands. But it's too late. The germs have already been placed on his penis. And he'll take this same germ ridden penis home and have sex with his lady, spreading his germs all over her. Women wonder why they're getting infections all the time. Moral of the story, "Men wash your hands before and after you use the restroom. It could save lives, and countless trips to the doctor's office."

There is so much that men don't know because they were never taught. It's not the man's fault if he's never been taught. You can't expect a German Shepard to be a good guard dog if he's never been trained, it's not realistic. But ignorance is no excuse. As a Player, it is your responsibility to seek out the knowledge necessary to play the game and take care of yourself to the best of your ability. Knowing thyself encompasses maintaining a confidence that exudes your masculinity. Too many Players are leaning on the woman and not standing on their own two feet. A Player must first recognize that his body is a temple, and understand that a Player never defiles the temple. You can't pollute the temple with garbage and expect it to stand strong. Maintain your swagger at all times! Learn how to care for yourself, and you will be able to care for your woman and win the game.

CHAPTER 8

TECHNOLOGY COWARDS

A Player's greatest weapon is his ability to talk. He can't truly exercise that weapon over the phone or texting. Thus, a Player's primary focus should be meeting with his woman and talking to her face-to-face. Women love and respect a man they can look at during a conversation. Eye-to-eye contact is mandatory when speaking with a woman. If she can't see you, it's hard for her to respect you, and this is why modern-day women are controlling relationships. You are allowing her to communicate with you via phone, text, email, etc., which makes it easier for her to display her emotions. Take her out of that comfort zone; it's not healthy for a relationship, and it takes the power away from the Player.

Imagine a lion in the jungle announcing over a loud-speaker that he desires a lioness. She would keep it moving and lose total respect for his authority. A lioness wants a lion who can roar to her face.

Cell phones are destroying relationships. Couples are meeting and leaving each other via their cell phones. Text messaging is the worst invention to ever infiltrate the Player game – they are totally emotionless. Do you really know what the person is saying via text message? You do not. Players don't get caught up in text messages. If you didn't say it, it didn't happen. Do you even know who's texting you?

The way to a woman's heart is through immediate contact, face-to-face discussion, touching, and visual expression. True Players do not use technology to talk for them; we talk for ourselves. The most significant part of the Player's game is his ability to communicate with his lady. Today's man has lost this art of divine communication. Divine communication is the language between a man and a woman that's innate, expressive, sincere, and passionate. Divine communication cannot be expressed through a cell phone. We're letting modern-day technology lead us astray.

No disrespect meant to the multi-millionaire men that have designed the smart phones, on-line dating, Skype, Facebook, etc. These clever guys have lured 95% of men to their world, a world that says you don't have to be who you truly are, that promises you can become anyone your imagination conjures up, as long as you remain hidden behind the deceptive screen of technology. Take a look at the inventors of these mechanisms. Most of them are squares (nerds) that couldn't get a date with a hot woman if they paid for it. Not because they aren't nice looking guys, but because they can't hold a conversation with a woman. They have no game. When you have no game, you hide behind technology.

Let's take a look at some of our most beloved superheroes, i.e., Spiderman, Superman, Iron Man, Captain America, and Bat Man. All of these characters, and basically every superhero you can think of, hide behind a costume. Why? Because most of them are shy wimps until they put these costumes on and are completely transformed. Does this mean that Superman isn't Superman without his cape and bright blue cat suit? Society is training the man to hide his true self behind a phony persona.

Why do you think most men only have the courage to approach women in dark clubs, under the influence of alcohol and sometimes even drugs? Most men possess little to no daylight courage. But True Players will approach a woman at ten in the morning, in a brightly-lit Starbucks or Target, without a second doubt. Players don't hide; we ride through the daylight, approaching all women in sight.

Technology allows cowards to be heroes, and without

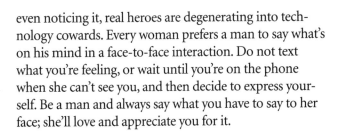

even noticing it, real heroes are degenerating into technology cowards. Every woman prefers a man to say what's on his mind in a face-to-face interaction. Do not text what you're feeling, or wait until you're on the phone when she can't see you, and then decide to express yourself. Be a man and always say what you have to say to her face; she'll love and appreciate you for it.

You will often meet women who hide behind technology because technology allows them to be uninhibited. She doesn't want you to think she's the freak that she really is, for fear that you will reject her or lose respect for her, so she uses technology to express her most intimate self. It's up to you, the Player, to lead her away from technology, and make her feel comfortable enough to deal with you face-to-face. Think about it - a woman will send you a picture of her naked body via MMS, but she's ashamed or coy about undressing in front of you. As a True Player, you must allow your woman to see and experience firsthand the pleasure that you take in sharing intimacy, rather than simulating intimacy via technology.

There are huge advantages to dealing with a person of interest face-to-face. You get the opportunity to read one another's energy. Your words can't be misleading or misconstrued, like they often are in a text exchange. You get to look at the woman eye-to-eye, and there's nothing sexier to a woman than a man gazing into her eyes during a conversation.

NO TEXTING

Texting = no emotions, no facial expressions, and no eye-to-eye contact. There is nothing more disturbing than a man who spends countless hours texting every woman in his circle. Pick up the damn phone and make a call if you can't meet face-to-face. Texting is very impersonal and it sends the message that you can't articulate yourself in a conversation with a woman. A grown man spending hours a day force-feeding his massive thumbs on a tiny cell phone keypad is unacceptable and highly disrespectful to the Player's game. If this act of non-verbal treason continues, you may be brought up on charges. Players communicate and take pride in verbalizing our thoughts.

NO FACEBOOK

Facebook is the devil. Facebook started off as a wonderful second option to Myspace. Now it's blossomed into the #1 social networking site in the world. Do I hate Facebook? I don't. Do I think it's weakening the Player's game? I do.

Facebook users have bought into the hype. It went from being a user-friendly way of contacting your loved ones and finding friends you haven't seen since the first grade, to people getting verbosely abused and killed. Facebook has caused more breakups in the past three years than cell phone-checking has done in the last ten years. People are truer to Facebook than they are to themselves.

I recently met a couple going through a divorce because the woman spent more time on Facebook than she did with her husband. She wasted 4-6 hours a day on Facebook gossiping with friends and family. Now that's a true addiction.

Let's look at another scenario where Facebook has wreaked havoc on a relationship. Rick and Yasmine had been maintaining a long-distance relationship for two years. It wasn't serious due to the distance, but both agreed it had a lot of potential. Before he left home to catch a flight to Ohio to visit Yasmine, Rick posted a Facebook status expressing his excitement at being in Ohio, even though he wasn't technically there yet. Unfortunately, Rick's flight was delayed, and he didn't land until the morning. He didn't call Yasmine to let her know about the delay, and when he didn't call her as promised that night, she went on his Facebook page and read his status. Yasmine lost her cool and assumed that Rick had ditched her, and was out with another woman. She wouldn't take his calls in the morning, and when they finally spoke, they were unable to mend the rift that arose from the miscommunication. All because the parties were playing the Facebook game rather than the Player's game.

ONLINE DATING SITES

According to recent studies, online dating sites are vastly becoming the wave of the future. This is absurd. The cowards are taking human interaction and making a mockery of it. Realistically, can you get to know someone on paper? Absolutely not! Americans have become lazy and unresponsive to basic human needs. A Player, true to the game, will go out of his house and into the streets to introduce himself to the lady he desires. This cowardly dating has gone too far. Before long, we'll begin to substitute real food with a pill (Jetsons cartoon) and live our lives totally through a computer. We are people of God, and the nature of man and woman must be upheld. Open your eyes and see that you're being manipulated into total dependence on technology, and growing more distant from your true nature. There's nothing more romantic than a man and a woman getting to know one another while walking through the park, or even having tea at a local Starbucks.

Think about it this way - if you have a relationship questionnaire in front of you that asks you to describe yourself, are you more likely to embellish or take the honest route? It's in your nature to make yourself look better than you are, but if you're face-to-face, the opportunity for embellishment is less likely. Hiding behind technology takes away your innate ability to be who you truly are. Players, i.e., real men, will take any and every opportunity to go out and meet and greet real women.

Top 5 places you can meet quality women in your area.

1. *Target or Walmart*
2. *Neighborhood grocery stores*
3. *Drug stores (Walgreens, Rite-Aid, etc.)*
4. *Starbucks or local tea and coffee cafés*
5. *Dine-in restaurants (Olive Garden, Houston's, Denny's, Outback Steakhouse, etc.)*

3 things that all true Players must know about locating and meeting women.

1. *Women love to eat*
2. *Women need to shop*
3. *Women always visit the drug store*

PHONE ETTIQUETTE

It's hard to say when it started, but the unfortunate reality is that men don't know the rules of engagement when it comes to telephone usage. Before the invention of voice mail and cell phones, it was considered customary for a man to call a woman and to continue calling until she answered the phone. With the invention of the voice mail and caller ID, men have gotten lazy, and laziness is un-Player like.

When you call a lady (during respectful hours of the day) and she doesn't answer, it's common courtesy to leave her a message. Players don't say, "I called and I didn't leave a message because I knew you would see my name in your caller ID." That's a total cop out. True Players don't rely on visual technology; they rely on their own voices.

As a Player, you should always want your lady to hear your voice. Anything repeated a significant number of times becomes a habit. Case in point, if you call your lady and constantly leave her messages when she's not available, your voice pattern becomes a part of her emotional psyche, and thus you become a habit that she must feed.

Think about it this way, Player. If a woman whispers in your ear, "You're the man, big daddy," how does that make you feel? Good, I hope. Every time you see her, you'll think to yourself, "I'm big daddy." There's a sense of confidence that develops when those words are orally expressed. If she writes down the exact same words, "You're the man, big daddy," it doesn't have nearly the same effect. You'll appreciate it, but you won't internalize it. If you want your woman to feel you and appreciate you, leave a damn message when you call.

After leaving a message, it's important to remember that you don't have to call again until she returns your call. There's nothing more annoying to a Queen than a man calling her all the time. As a Player, the rule of thumb is one call, one message. If she's interested, she'll get back to you as soon as she has a minute; trust me. If she doesn't call you back, give her a few days before calling again. If she still doesn't respond, trash the number. Don't be insulted or angry; just appreciate that when one door closes another will open. No woman is worth you losing yourself over. There's always another woman waiting for a man that she can appreciate.

WHEN TO USE TECHNOLOGY

Technology should be used only when necessary. When there is no way you can meet face-to-face, pick up the phone, and when you're not able to use the phone, only then is texting an option. And for the love of God, when you text, spell out your words and spell them correctly. You can hide ignorance through face-to-face conversation, but not when it's spelled out right before your eyes.

Don't take the gift of human interaction for granted; it's the most genuine and acceptable form of communication for a woman. Players don't text each other, they talk to one another. As a man, get out of the practice of texting other men; it's unacceptable, unless it's your only option. You can text your woman, but make it short and sweet, and only use texts at times when a phone call isn't possible.

Earpiece

The phone earpiece is an accessory that's not becoming of a Player. You only need an earpiece when you're driving or your hands are occupied. Women find a man walking around with a bug-like earpiece protruding from his ear unattractive. Can you blame them? Earpieces are definitely a no-no when you're in the club. If you have business to discuss, do it before you enter the club or party. Once you're in the club or at a social gathering, it's time to mingle. Leave your earpiece in the car.

CHAPTER 9

CLUB ETTIQUETTE

The nightclub is the Player's playground, where real men come to enjoy the unlimited eye candy, and to score home runs and win the game. It is also where most potential-Players are judged, and given their biggest stamp of approval or disapproval. Women usually outnumber men three to one in a nightclub, granting Players ample opportunity to make a mark on the Player game. There's something about the darkness of the club and the constant downpour of alcohol that gives potential-Players the courage of ten warriors.

The clubs are a gift and a curse. The gift is all the beautiful treats (beautiful women) that have come out to play the game. The curse is that most of the women in the club have more game than the average potential-Players approaching them.

Women (Prolific Players) come out for one purpose and one purpose only: men. Don't let her innocent smile and bashful eyes fool you; she's fully aware of everything going on around her. She knows that her outfit, perfume, walk, stance, etc. are attracting your attention. A woman will accent the part of her body that draws the most admiration. If she has full lips, she will probably have on thick gloss to make them glisten. If she has nice breasts, she will compliment them accordingly, by way of bras that boost and clothes that cling. If her ass is her centerpiece, she'll have on booty-hugging jeans or a stretchy dress. Women are not stupid. She knows what you like and what you're attracted to, and she will stop at nothing to get your attention, if your attention is her desire.

So if women are coming to the nightclub to attract men, and men are coming to the nightclub to choose women, what's the problem? Easy answer: men are trying too hard and instead of attracting the woman, men are sending her running in the opposite direction. Isn't it amazing that the same super stud walks into the same club every week and garners the same high level of attention, while the weak man watches in admiration, wishing he could be the other man for just one night? There's a reason the super stud constantly outperforms the super dud. The super stud doesn't come to the club searching and praying for attention, it's given to him automatically. He's simply being himself and the women love it. The super dud goes out of his way to get attention, mimicking the studs, or something he saw on TV, and usually ends up going home alone. You are a super dud if you:

1. *Spend more than 30 minutes to get ready for a party;*
2. *Are jealous-hearted and concern yourself with the attention another man is receiving;*
3. *Assassinate the characters of other men;*
4. *Gossip;*
5. *Find that girls constantly give you the wrong number;*
6. *Crave attention;*
7. *Go home and masturbate once you leave the club; that's just non-sense.*

Of the seven stated, number two is probably the worst. True Players are only concerned about what's going on in their lane. What the next man eats doesn't make you shit, so don't be worried about what he chooses to ingest. Jealousy is truly a female trait. If you possess this unmanly trait, check yourself.

Gossiping is the second worst behavior for a Player to engage in, as well as the most female of all emasculating tendencies. Men don't gossip and men don't hate on one another. Keep your mouth closed or it'll get closed by a True Player. If you don't have anything good to say about the next man, don't say anything at all. Men congratulate one another, they don't emasculate each other.

Craving attention is the trait that deters most women. Women love a man of mystery and mystique. Women want the men they can't figure out, the men they can never have. A woman is always drawn to the man who doesn't go out of his way to impress her or catch her attention. And a True Player knows that the man with patience and perseverance wins the race.

Women love what they can't have and they love not being noticed; it's a challenge to their game. Most women will go out of their way to attract you, especially if they feel they can have you without much effort. Players get approached, while non-Players beg to be approached. It has nothing to do with your look, and everything to do with your confidence and knowledge of the game. Test my theory. Look a woman in her eyes and tell her she's beautiful. Before she can respond, walk away. When you see her again she'll appreciate you and respect you more. She may even chase you down. Women love compliments, but what they love more is a man who compliments without expecting a number and a conversation in return. If she's obviously interested or pursuing you, naturally you don't need to test this theory. But if she's not, the walk-away technique is a good way to pique her interest, and possibly even her desire.

CHAPTER 10

LEAD HER

There's nothing sexier to a woman than a virile man who knows how to take a woman and lead her in an appealing direction. On the contrary, there's nothing more despicable than a man who allows his woman to lead him around, forcing her into the role of the lion while he prances around like the lioness.

In every organization, be it a business, club, place of worship, animal kingdom, etc., there's always a leader (alpha male). Someone has to be appointed as director, otherwise the group will eventually suffer and crumble. The Player is that leader.

Despite what a woman may say, no woman wants a man that she can lead, or mislead. Nor does a woman want a man she can walk all over and boss around. And no woman wants a relationship that's 50/50. Just as a woman brings nurturing to a relationship, a man must bring leadership. If a Player doesn't take control, then he's not a True Player, and the woman isn't interested for very long.

It's not in the woman's nature to lead the man. For example, a man and woman are walking down the street holding hands amorously, without a care in the world. Suddenly a Pit Bull comes bounding toward them with one thing on his mind: destroy. What's the nature of the woman and the man in this instance? Naturally, the woman will scream and instinctively cower behind the man while the man, although equally terrified, will in most cases respond by placing himself in immediate danger in order to shield and protect the woman. Moral of the story is, if you have a woman that screams 50/50, ask her to take half the bites.

Women feel entitled to more authority in relationships because they're making more money and a lot of them are supervisors/owners at their prospective companies. Player, you cannot let a woman lead you, no matter how much money she makes. If she's leading you, that means she has no respect for you. Sometimes a woman will go out of her way to find a chump (non-Player) to lead, so she can feel empowered. This is not because she enjoys leading a man around, but likely because she's seeking revenge. Revenge? Yes, sir. The man before you probably mistreated her and made her feel inferior and insecure about her life decisions. Even though this man is gone from her life, the feeling of nothingness and abandonment has not left her aching heart. When she meets the next man, who is smitten, she destroys his self-confidence by mistreating him in response to the pain she still feels from her previous relationship. And so a viscous cycle begins. A True Player will stop the cycle before it starts.

Rule of thumb: never date a woman who hasn't been out of a serious relationship for at least a year (12 months). Most women hold onto baggage for an inordinate amount of time, and it usually takes a year or so for the woman to heal her heart. Throughout that year she will date and mistreat other men until her heart feels better. You don't want to be that probation guy. She uses the probation guy(s) until a Real Player comes along.

Player, once you meet a woman, the sure way to find out if she's bitter about a previous break-up is to listen to her. Women love to talk and if you listen to a woman long enough she'll reveal everything you want to know. Another rule of thumb: don't ask a lot of questions. A woman (Prolific Player) will wear any disguise she thinks pleases you, but she can't wear the disguise if you keep your mouth shut and hold your cards close. So don't ask a lot of questions. While you're asking a lot of questions and revealing your cards, she's evaluating you, deciphering your every desire, strength, and weakness. The more she knows about you, the more control she'll have over you.

As the leader, you can't take advantage and mislead or mistreat the woman. A woman will trust your lead initially (80% of the time), but once you prove you can't handle the steering wheel, she'll push you out and take control forever. Players, you must be accountable, responsible, and dependable at all times.

1. **Accountable** - *Be where you're supposed to be when you're supposed to be there.*
2. **Responsible** - *If you say it, you must do it. A Player is only as strong as his word.*
3. **Dependable** - *99.9% of the time, she has to know she can rely on you, and that even if you can't come through, you'll die trying.*

Each number is synonymous with the other, and all three make for a well-appreciated Player.

A huge part (95%) of taking the lead entails you knowing your woman. You can't influence a woman unless you have an idea of where she wants to be led, and the only way you will ever know how to lead her is to observe her.

As a Player, you must take the time to notice everything about your woman. Not by asking questions, but by observing and taking note of what she says, what she likes, what she dislikes, what makes her laugh, what makes her angry, etc. It's not a hard job, and it should be an enjoyment.

Women leave very little to secret. If she likes you, she'll invite you into her world and disclose all there is to know about her. This disclosure will not happen overnight, so you must be patient. When she sees you're an active listener (the ability to listen without interruption and to regurgitate what was said) and that you appear to care, she'll give you the combination to her debit card and the password to her Facebook account. Not that you need either, but this is her way of showing you she values and appreciates you.

The best example I can provide to illuminate what it means for a Player to take the lead is the story of a beautiful woman named Pamela, an attorney working in Los Angeles. Smart, witty, confident and tired of the dating scene, Pamela agreed to a blind date with a friend of a friend, Sebastian, who was also an attorney. During dinner they had intelligent conversation, and weary, wary Pamela began to trust Sebastian, largely due to his persistent eye contact and the sincerity he displayed not only while speaking to her but also while listening to her. They went out dancing

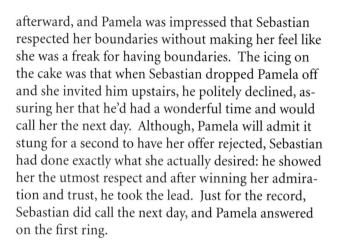

afterward, and Pamela was impressed that Sebastian respected her boundaries without making her feel like she was a freak for having boundaries. The icing on the cake was that when Sebastian dropped Pamela off and she invited him upstairs, he politely declined, assuring her that he'd had a wonderful time and would call her the next day. Although, Pamela will admit it stung for a second to have her offer rejected, Sebastian had done exactly what she actually desired: he showed her the utmost respect and after winning her admiration and trust, he took the lead. Just for the record, Sebastian did call the next day, and Pamela answered on the first ring.

But do note, it's asinine for Player to think he can get a woman to believe in him enough to let him take the lead when he has absolutely nothing to stand on. A Real Player is accountable, responsible and most of all he's virile. A Player has a job and makes money to take care of his responsibilities. A Player has a place to live, a car to drive, a steady job, and money in his pocket. Don't ever confuse a Player for a Pimp. Although all Real Players respect the doctrine of Pimps, we do not subscribe to making a living by soliciting women for money and ungodly gains.

CHAPTER 11

FATHERHOOD

Taking care of your children is your greatest strength; not taking care of your children is your greatest fault. The greatest gift our Father above has given us is the gift of life. As a man, you have inherited and control that gift here on earth. It is your responsibility to ensure our planet continues to populate with the healthiest and strongest seeds available. As a leader of our world, it's your job to make certain your seed is given the very best you have to offer.

A responsible and loving father is an aphrodisiac to a woman. Women get turned on by the mere thought of a responsible man, hoping that the loyalty and dedication you express toward your children will be paralleled in your romantic relationships.

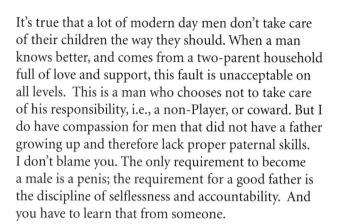

It's true that a lot of modern day men don't take care
of their children the way they should. When a man
knows better, and comes from a two-parent household
full of love and support, this fault is unacceptable on
all levels. This is a man who chooses not to take care
of his responsibility, i.e., a non-Player, or coward. But I
do have compassion for men that did not have a father
growing up and therefore lack proper paternal skills.
I don't blame you. The only requirement to become
a male is a penis; the requirement for a good father is
the discipline of selflessness and accountability. And
you have to learn that from someone.

It's a known fact that most young men shy away from
their responsibilities when it comes to fatherhood,
not because they don't love the child, but because they
don't love themselves. When you don't have a father
figure in your life, it's very difficult for you to understand and appreciate the role of being a father. Bottom
line, it's difficult to make a copy when you don't have
the original.

Potential-Players, I know you think it's admirable at
times for you to have better things to do than spend
time with your child. This is not Player-like, and it's
degrading and disrespectful to God's kingdom. In the
right order of things, you must nurture every seed you
plant. If not, you will face a wrath much greater than
you can ever imagine. Remember, children are always

protected by God's embrace and if you abandon them, He will abandon you.

Money vs. Time Spent

The cowardly way out for non-Players has always been the easy excuse. The non-Player would say to the judge in court, "I don't have any money. I can't afford to spend time with my child." This excuse is unacceptable and ignorant. Most men don't know that a child would rather have you in his/her life without a dime, as opposed to you showering them with money and gifts to compensate for your physical and emotional absence. Spending quality time with your child is the greatest love you can give to him/her. It's never about money or gifts, but about the love you give. A walk, a day in the park, a movie night in your home cost very little.

Even if you don't like the mother of your child, don't neglect that child. It's not the child's fault. That child didn't choose its mother or father; that child didn't even choose to be born. You chose that child, and now you must provide him/her with love, support, and a positive example.

Baby Mama Drama

Players, it's very important that you know the woman you're laying with. It doesn't take much for a woman to flip sides on you, especially when she feels betrayed or belittled. Many women won't hesitate to use the

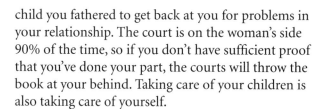

child you fathered to get back at you for problems in your relationship. The court is on the woman's side 90% of the time, so if you don't have sufficient proof that you've done your part, the courts will throw the book at your behind. Taking care of your children is also taking care of yourself.

Often, a Player will encounter a woman asking for child support beyond what she needs to take care of that child. Some women demand name brand clothing, the most technologically-advanced toys, and expensive vacations. This has nothing to do with the child, and everything to do with the child's mother being disgruntled with you because you're not with her. So she plays with your emotions by taking you to court. Players, know this and know it well - there's not a judge alive who will sentence you if you can show that you've been spending adequate time with your child. You will only get punished for being a negligent parent if you are actually neglecting your child. There will be no repercussions if you genuinely don't have extra money to pay for luxury items the baby doesn't really need. Keep and maintain all of your receipts. And make sure you are giving your child everything he or she needs and deserves to the very best of your ability.

If you are unemployed and can't afford to take care of your child, go to the City Hall nearest you and file paperwork to let the courts know that you're looking for work and that you will continue to take care of your responsibilities as best you can until you find employment. If the woman goes to the court before you, she can make your life very uncomfortable.

Despite how upset you may get, you will not raise your hand to hit a woman. Players realize that men are physically dominant over women, and it's absolutely wrong to use that to their advantage. Learn to dominate your woman with your mind, not your fist. Hitting a woman is a cowardly act.

Always think two steps ahead of your woman. She's constantly planning your rise and demise. To be a Player is to be smart, to be smart means you must be knowledgeable, and to be knowledgeable means you must read and utilize your resources.

Bottom line, every man who has enough energy to lay down with a woman and impregnate her with his seed should have the wherewithal to take care of the baby and her, in that order.

And if you have a meddling mother or family member getting in the way and giving you bad advice, tell them to mind their business. Remember, your mama means well, but she can't go to jail for you. The best advice you can ever get is the motto every Player lives by:

"Players don't run away from responsibilities; we run to them."

Don't be afraid of loving your child.

CHAPTER 12

GUILTY PLEASURES

According to Wikipedia, a guilty pleasure is "something one enjoys and considers pleasurable despite feeling guilt for enjoying it."

Masturbating, pornography, Viagra and strip clubs are the four items on my list of guilty pleasures that most men enjoy.

MASTERBATING

Should men masturbate? Absolutely not! According to the Tao of Sexology, when the average male ejaculates, he loses about one tablespoon of semen. According to scientific research, the nutritional value of this amount of semen is equal to that of two pieces of New York steak, ten eggs, six oranges and two lemons combined. That includes proteins, vitamins, minerals, amino acids - in short, everything. The book goes on to say that the precise word should be "going" not "coming" because everything—the erection, vital energy, millions of live sperms, hormones, nutrients, even a little of the man's personality—disappears.

Players don't need to masturbate and they shouldn't masturbate. There is a level of discipline that comes with being a True Player, and if you want to master the woman, you must first master yourself. The idea of taking your imagination to a foreign and imaginary place to gain sexual satisfaction is absurd. As a Player, you must preserve this energy for your lady. If you don't have a lady, wait until you find a woman and enjoy the release of pleasure with her, not your hand.

Most men will tell you that they take pride in masturbating, while they don't actually know why they do it, and they don't understand the consequences of their actions. If you have enough time to conjure up an imaginary woman, you have enough time to go out and meet one.

Players, we must first realize that sex is meant for the purpose of pro-creation, not recreation. But most of us choose to indulge because we love the feelings of power and pleasure that it brings us. When you masturbate, which leaves no chance for pro-creation, the Godliness that should be enjoyed by a man and woman is diminished. It detracts from your true inner-self, that the self that naturally craves the attention and affection of a woman. When you have an orgasm and you only have your pillow and lubricant beside you in bed, well that's just sad. Have patience and discipline and your next orgasm (with a flesh and blood woman) will be well worth the wait.

Most men will argue that sometimes they don't feel like dealing with a woman but they do need to ejacu-late. That's a cop out and a cowardly excuse to play with yourself without feeling lame. The penis has an all-seeing eye for a reason, and that reason is to enjoy the journey of being inside of a woman's warmth, not the palm of your hand.

When you feel the urge to have an orgasm and you don't have a lady nearby, go to the gym, go running, pick up a book and read. Use that energy construc-tively, not foolishly.

PORNOGRAPHY
Easily one of the greatest male pastimes, pornography racks in billions of dollars annually. In 2002, there were 467 Hollywood films released and 11,303 adult films released. This gives you an idea of how many men are enjoying the pleasures of adult films.

As a Player, it's important to remember that everything you create for you and your woman should have your signature on it. When you indulge in porn, you're allowing imaginary external stimuli to become a part of your sexual evolution and experience. Most men who indulge in porn are chronic masturbators and are not easily satisfied by the average woman. We've become obsessed with Hollywood's version of a beautiful woman. Concentrate on and appreciate the real woman you're fortunate enough to have in bed beside you, and your sex life together will become better than any adult film.

As a result of exposure to this false imagery, some men will need to think of women they've seen in a porn flick when they're having sex with their real, flesh and blood Queens. True Players don't need external stimuli to get excited about women; all we need is natural body-to-body contact. That's why it's very important that you find a woman you're attracted to on all levels – body, mind, and spirit. There's nothing more demoralizing to a woman that having a man who's sleeping with her, but not actually attracted to her.

VIAGARA
Unless you have a prescription from a physician due to medical reasons, there's no excuse for any man to use sexual enhancement drugs. You are a sexual coward if you use Viagra, Cialis, etc. The reason men

are using sex drugs is that they want to enhance their performance in bed. Men, if you're having issues in the bedroom, there are safer and healthier options for you than a pill.

The key to loving a woman in the bed is taking your time. The average man thinks that the harder and rougher he is, the more she likes it. Wrong! Most women prefer a man with a gentle stroke as opposed to you pounding her canvas with your brush. Lovemaking is an art (an art that we'll discuss in detail in Volume II) that every man is capable of mastering. The first rule of thumb is to be with a woman that you admire, respect, and enjoy. Second rule is to be in shape both physically and mentally so you can perform adequately in the bedroom without losing interest or breath.

Men, if you need to build stamina, go to the gym or work out at home instead of popping a little blue pill. The side effects of enhancement drugs alone should deter you from such an act. Popping the pill is equivalent to using express mail rather than regular mail. Express mail arrives faster, but there's a higher price to pay. Running a few days a week or even walking will build your stamina and while you may not notice the difference immediately, your progress will be slow, steady, and permanent. Remember, the best sex you can have, is natural sex. NO PILLS!

STRIP CLUBS

Stop wasting your money on something that gives you nothing in return. I truly respect the profession of adult entertainment, but I don't see the pleasure in spending money you don't have on a fantasy. It would be different if the woman dancing for you was guaranteed to be in your bed at the night's end, but that's not the case. Instead, you end up spending a boatload of money on alcohol and lap dances just to go home and masturbate, or have lackluster sex with your woman while thinking about the dancer at the strip club.

It's really quite illogical if you think about it. Players, spend your money where it counts the most. Don't work hard all week just to waste it on a fantasy. Use that money to sign your lady up for a pole dancing class or exotic Pilates. Create your own adult entertainment in the comfort of your own home.

CHAPTER 13

CHIVALRY

Before we even begin this conversation, if you don't know the meaning of the word chivalry, read carefully: the sum of the ideal qualifications of a man, including courtesy, generosity, and valor.

The quickest non-communicative way to impress a woman is through your chivalrous acts. As Players, it's an unwritten mandate that you extend complete and sincere courtesy, generosity, and valor to all women, all the time.

It complements your manhood when you extend your courtesy to assist a woman. She's physically inferior to you and relies on your strength in many cases. If you see a woman carrying an obviously heavy item, it's only right that you run over and assist her. Players should always open the door for a woman, and let her walk through first. Even if you have to stand there for a few extra seconds, it's your responsibility to do so.

You may think, why? If we're equal, she should hold her own door. True, but not true. If it were your mother or grandmother needing assistance, would you want a man to assist or ignore her? Show the same courtesy to an unknown woman on the street that you would show your mother. I agree that there are some women that don't appreciate your chivalrous acts, but we'll excuse these viragos for their boorish ingratitude. There are women in the world that weren't taught to appreciate their role, just as there are men who weren't taught to appreciate theirs. Don't let the few ruin it for the rest.

Men and women both have important spiritual, bio-logical, and sociological roles to play in this society. Players should honor, respect, protect, and preserve the women of this world. A Player's closest connection to God is through a woman; if you find a man who doesn't respect women, it's also true that he doesn't respect God.

PLAYER'S ANTHEM

The Player's anthem is the unwritten code of all Players. It is an oath to one's self that every Player must accept and honor. Once indoctrinated into this elite club, which offers life-time membership, you must swear to abide by the rules and regulations of this circle, the Player's Circle.

You are becoming a part of something that is distinguished, respected and also shunned by the misfits in our society. An important note that you must make to self is that just because you have finished reading the content of this book, you have not gained automatic acceptance into the Player's Circle. You now have to put all you have learned into action and behave like a True Player. Remember, to be a Player is to know how to treat a woman the right way.

To be officially accepted, you must write a two to five page synopsis expressing your understanding of the content of this book, and send it to the following address:

Attn: Player's Circle
645 W. 9th Street 110-281
Los Angeles, CA. 90015

After your synopsis is reviewed and accepted, you'll receive a stamp of approval from a group of elite Royal Players. This stamp of approval let's you know that you have what it takes to become a certified Player.

This acceptance isn't something you brag about to your friends, or make a mockery of to those who don't posses this card. Instead, you keep your mouth shut and your game tight and use this card to promote your inner self.

The anthem is simple, and you should recite it everyday before you step outside. The anthem is called the "The 10 Plays to Becoming a Player."

The 10 Plays to Becoming a Player

1. *Always be courteous to all women.*
2. *Always rescue a damsel in distress.*
3. *Always refer to a woman by her name and nothing less.*
4. *Be gentle and understanding to all women.*
5. *Never walk by a beautiful woman without acknowledging her.*
6. *Respect a woman for her mind and not her body.*
7. *Always honor thy word, and be dependable, reliable, and on time.*
8. *Call a woman during respectful hours.*
9. *Always make a good first impression.*
10. *Always look, dress, and smell your best to impress the best.*

King Play: Only approach women with the purest of intentions. And remember, stay in your lane.

10 POINT CHECK BEFORE YOU LEAVE THE HOUSE (EVERY DAY)

1. *Take a shower.*
2. *Brush your teeth, floss, use mouthwash, and stick a pack of gum in your pocket.*
3. *Brush or comb your hair.*
4. *Put on clean underwear.*
5. *Put on clean clothes and shoes.*
6. *Apply body oils or cologne.*
7. *Make sure your wallet has ID and at least $20 cash in it.*
8. *Write down your itinerary for the day.*
9. *Look in the mirror for a once-over before you leave.*
10. *Tell yourself "I am the man, and I was made to be who I am."*

UN-WRITTEN RULES OF PLAYERHOOD

1. *Always open a door for a lady.*
2. *Never sit with your back to the door when on a date.*
3. *Always position yourself on the outside of your woman, closest to the aisle in the movies, closest to the road and traffic when outdoors, etc. You need to be in a position of protection at all times.*
4. *Never let a woman walk to her car alone, especially when it's dark.*
5. *Always walk a lady to her door and make sure she's safe.*
6. *Pay a woman compliments on her physical appearance.*
7. *Learn to prepare your girl's favorite meal. Women love men that can cook, but don't do it too often; just enough to make her appreciate it.*
8. *When visiting your lady's home, always take out her garbage and always let the toilet seat down when you're finish with your business..*
9. *Pay attention to how a woman treats her friends; she will treat you the same way.*
10. *Keep your home clean and presentable at all times.*
11. *Always have cocktails or drinks available for your woman at your house.*
12. *Light candles and incense when your girl come over.*

13. *Keep your woman laughing and smiling; if you don't, another man will.*

14. *Don't have your male friends over when your woman is there.*

15. *Never put a woman second to video games. Grow up!*

16. *Always appreciate your woman and never take her for granted. Women need attention.*

17. *Don't take relationship advice from friends who aren't True Players.*

18. *Buy your lady a card, flowers, candy, etc. at least once a month.*

19. *Don't argue with your woman; you can't win. State your point and keep it moving.*

20. *Keep your hands and nails clean at all times.*

21. *When talking to a woman, always look her in the eyes.*

22. *Never ask a woman about her past relationships. Be in her present, and build a future together.*

23. *Read the books, As a Man Thinketh and Secrets Men Keep.*

24. *Don't criticize your woman, coach her. She wants to learn how to be the woman you desire. Be careful; she must be the right woman from the very start.*

25. *Take your woman couple's dancing (Chicago-Stepping, Salsa, Ballroom, etc.). Couples should hang around other couples. And dancing is fun, intimate, and always sexy.*

A Final Note

It's in a woman's nature to do for you, and to make sure you're happy. If she's not doing this for you, it's highly probable that she's bringing happiness to another man. If you're not feeling totally satisfied in your relationship, more than likely you're the sucker, not the Player. A woman aims to please, and if you're not doing your job to receive her goodness, she's probably laying next to me (a Real Player), when you think she's at work. Holler!

G.O.M.A.B.

Player Quotes

How many times have you heard,"Don't hate the player,hate the game?" That's exactly what it is. A game. Any half way decent looking man with a little bit going for himself will consider himself a Player because he has choices. In this game of choice you play the field until you're able to make a decision. I call the decision making process the rite of passage. You are a real man when your maturity reaches a stage where you can focus on one woman and maintain this thing we call a relationship, or marriage. That's when you find your inner MVP. Don't let the word Player disgust you. If you feel like you're being played, get yourself into the championship ring and make the choice to win the MVP. Real Players play to Win!

~ *Myron "Magic" Giggua.*

A Player exudes confidence and is self-assured. He doesn't care what people think about him - good or bad. He just is and he knows it.

~ *Sebastian Wolski*

The word "Player" or "Playa" has so many definitions. Most people hear those words and automatically think, "cheating male or female." That's not so. A True Player has solid confidence within him or herself. True Players don't lie; it's not necessary. In the worst of situations, a true player understands that there's a right way to do wrong.

~ Pamela Kubeczka

A Player commands respect as the heart commands love.

~ Ricky Davis

You know you're a Player when the man won't stop begging for your time and space. You know he's trapped when he utters the words, "I'll do anything for you baby."

~ Laverne "Gu-Gu" Gray

Patience, positive and peace are what make a True Player. If you love yourself, you can love another. It's not about how many hearts you break, but how many hearts you fix and keep safe.

~ Annette White

A Player is an individual who takes care of his business in all aspects of life. His life experience garners him the love and respect of everyone he encounters. Original Players take homage in honoring their word. My word is as good as a block of gold, solid to the max. I'm an original player. I've been putting it down since Moby Dick was a Goldfish.

~ Shermaxx

ABOUT THE AUTHOR

Relationship therapist and television personality Dr. Tiy-E, more widely known as "The Relationship Prince," is a bestselling author, life-coach, playwright, educator and entrepreneur. Dr. Tiy-E's mission is to encourage others to find peace and love by establishing and sustaining healthy relationships. The answer is his latest installment: P.L.A.Y.E.R.'s Circle, his fifth and best venture to date.

Most recently seen on Bravo's, "The Real Housewives of Atlanta," Dr. Tiy-E's infectious personality has become a magnet for controversy and change. His 'no-holds barred' approach and proven methods are what landed him his television breakthrough as the Resident Relationship Expert on "The Ricki Lake Show." He has since appeared on hundreds of programs including, TBS's "The Real Gilligan's Island," "The Greg Berendt Show," TV One's "Baisden After Dark," " Good Morning Chicago," Bravo's "ManSwers," MTV's "Made," and BET's "My Black is Beautiful," to name a few. Dr. Tiy-E's relationship advice has also been featured in Cosmopolitan, Essence, Jet and Ebony magazines. He continues to give millions of women around the globe insight into how men really feel about love, relationships, intimacy, and commitment. Dr. Tiy-E undertakes a journey both universal and personal, and has laid groundbreaking work for the first of three relationship "Bibles."

Dr. Tiy-E is a member of Phi Beta Sigma Fraternity, Inc and Prince Hall Affiliated Masons. He currently resides in Los Angeles.

www.drtiye.com